space... the final frontier

Since early man gazed up at the sky for the very first time, the great unknown of space has held a very special fascination. Even the earliest civilisations studied movements of celestial objects, from the knowledge they gained came the crucial ability of time-keeping, a start to our understanding of the natural forces that affect us.

We have come a long way since then, from simple telescopes and early rockets to the Hubble space telescope and deep space probes, these help us to look further out into space.

The thought of man as a space traveller, for so long just a dream, has started to become a reality. In the last few decades we have ventured beyond the confines of our home planet – to walk on the moon, to live and work in space.

But where will our unquenchable thirst for knowledge take us?

Ed White, the first American to walk in space

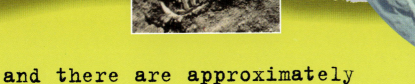

... and there are approximately 1,000 million stars (like our Sun) in each galaxy

early PIONEERS

The Polish astronomer Nikolas Copernicus (1473-1543)

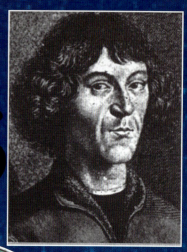

From the first civilisations

man has watched the stars and fantasised about travelling into space. The moon was an attractive goal, with a story written as early as 1638 by Domingo Gonsales describing a lunar mission, powered by swans! But it was Jules Verne in the late 19th century whose writing inspired, among others, the American Robert Goddard to believe that multi-stage rockets really could be made to reach the moon. Despite having his early ideas ridiculed by the press, Goddard perfected and launched a liquid-fuelled rocket in 1926 kicking off space missions for real.

Since the beginning of the century, on the other side of the world, a deaf Russian called Konstantin Tsiolkovsky had been researching the use of powered rockets for travelling to other planets. His suggestion of using liquid oxygen and liquid hydrogen was taken up by other scientists and proved successful.

Although serious research continued in Germany, with 87 experimental rocket launches by 1932, it was Willy Ley's emigration to the USA and his founding of the American Rocket Society which popularised the idea of space travel.

Another German, Wernher von Braun, began working with US scientists after the war, he felt convinced man could travel to the Moon.

He was the first person to believe that the Sun, not the Earth was at the centre of our Solar System

Explorer 1 heads for the skies

Konstantin Tsiolkovsky

Italian scientist Galileo (1564-1642) pioneered the use of the telescope ...

TO TRAVEL BEYOND THE STARS HAS BEEN MAN'S DREAM FOR THOUSANDS OF YEARS ...

Sputnik 1

In 1955 the Russian's R-7 rocket was capable of launching a satellite into orbit, and a year later von Braun's US army team were able to launch their four-stage Jupiter rocket. In 1958 he successfully launched Explorer 1, America's first satellite, but this was one year after the Russians had amazed the world with Sputnik. Determined not to be outdone by the USSR again, the Americans created NASA, the National Aeronautics and Space Administration centre, and the 'Space Race' between USA and USSR began. The main objects were to get man to orbit the earth and eventually to put man on the moon.

SPACE FAX

SPUTNIK 1, launched on 4 October 1957 was the world's first artificial satellite.
It weighed 184lbs (83.5kgs) and orbited the earth at 17,500mph emitting "bleep" signals that tracking stations all over the world could hear.

... THAT DREAM WAS JUST ABOUT TO BECOME REALITY

Wernher von Braun

World War II V2 rocket

A dog called Laika was the first creature to orbit the earth; closely followed by Strelka and Belka.

Ham was the first chimp to fly in space

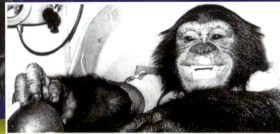

... he discovered mountains on our Moon and the four largest moons of Jupiter.

the space RACE

Yuri Gagarin – the first man in space

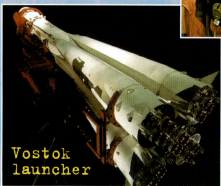

Valentina Tereshkova – the first woman in space

The winners of the first round were clearly the USSR. Their cosmonaut, Yuri Gagarin, became the first human in space when he was launched in a Vostok spacecraft on 12 April 1961 at 9.07am. After orbiting the Earth for just over an hour, at a speed of around five miles per second, he returned safely to worldwide fame. American scientists at NASA responded by declaring that they could and would, put their own men into orbit as soon as possible. Alan Shepard's May 1961 sub-orbital flight boosted morale, but the real change in people's expectations came when American

Vostok launcher

... TO PUT A MAN ON THE MOON AND RETURN HIM SAFELY TO EARTH ...

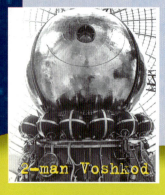

2-man Voshkod

THE MERCURY SEVEN — Back row l-r: Alan Shepard, Virgil Grissom, Gordon Cooper Front row, l-r: Walter Schirra, Donald Slayton, John Glenn, Scott Carpenter

Luna 9 probe sends back images from the Moon's surface in 1966.

President John F Kennedy vowed to *"put a man on the moon and return him safely to earth before this decade is out"*.

The Russians followed Gagarin's success with a 25-hour orbit by Gherman Titov, but better remembered is US astronaut John Glenn who, launched February 1962 in Friendship 7, orbited for nearly 5 hours and convinced the Americans that they could win the space race.

In the first half of the 1960s the USA's Mercury and Gemini missions made gains on their Russian rivals. While USSR's Alexei Leonov carried out the first space walk in 1965, the Gemini flights were practising space rendezvous, docking with astronauts spending long periods outside their craft.

1966 found both the USSR and USA preparing to send 3 man crews in lunar modules launched by powerful 3 stage rockets to the moon; USA with the Apollo program and USSR with Soyuz. Both teams suffered delays and setbacks. As the end of the decade approached, successful missions practised docking above the moon's surface and orbited the moon in safety.

Man was now just a few short step's from landing on the moon...

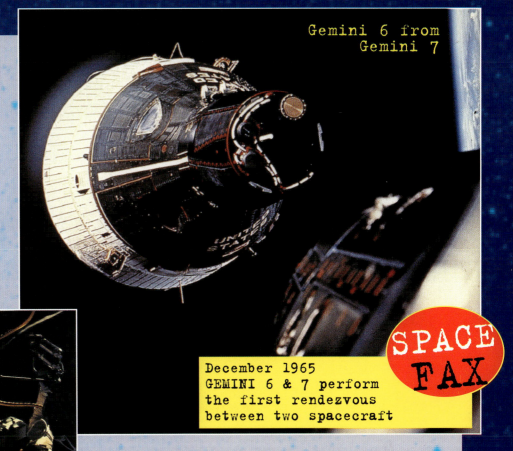

Gemini 6 from Gemini 7

Ed White is the first American to walk in space

December 1965
GEMINI 6 & 7 perform the first rendezvous between two spacecraft

SPACE FAX

Alan Shepard is spacebound in Mercury Redstone 3

Gemini 8 pilots David Scott and Neil Armstrong in their capsule after splashdown

In 1968, astronauts Frank Borman, Jim Lovell and Bill Anders orbit the Moon in Apollo 8.

man on the MOON

The crew of Apollo 11 (l-r) Neil Armstrong, Michael Collins and Buzz Aldrin

Man's first footprint on the Moon

In July 1969 disaster struck USSR's attempt to win the moon race. Their N1 rocket exploded just after take-off and destroyed the launch pad. This left the USA free to concentrate on their goal – to let a man walk on the moon before the end of the year.

On 16th July 1969 practically every TV in the world was tuned to the same TV broadcast, witnessing the giant Saturn V rocket propel Apollo 11, on its historic journey. Three days later, Neil Armstrong brought the lunar module down onto the moon's surface with only a few seconds of fuel to spare, the whole world cheered his words, "Houston, The Eagle has landed". History had truly been made.

Astronauts Armstrong and Aldrin spent 21 hours on the moon collecting rock samples, setting up experiments and sending TV pictures back to their amazed audience on earth. They even received a congratulatory phone call from US President Nixon!

After safely docking with and re-entering the command module Columbia, the three US astronauts returned to Earth and a heroes' welcome. They had to spend 3 weeks in quarantine, with some white mice for company to make sure they had not picked up any 'space bugs', before finally returning to their happy wives and families on 10th August 1969.

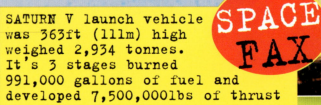

SPACE FAX

SATURN V launch vehicle was 363ft (111m) high weighed 2,934 tonnes. It's 3 stages burned 991,000 gallons of fuel and developed 7,500,000lbs of thrust

Over 600 million people worldwide saw Apollo 11 lift-off live on television.

Apollo 15: Jim Irwin, the Lunar Module and first Lunar Rover

'Earthrise'

Apollo service and command modules

After Apollo 11 six more missions flew to the moon, five of them successfully continuing the experiments started by Armstrong and Aldrin. The mission which did not land on the moon was the ill-fated Apollo 13, when an explosion in space, blew a hole in the side of the Service Module, threatening a disastrous end to the flight. The three brave astronauts, Lovell, Haise and Swigert, managed to coax the damaged craft home, to the relief of the watching world. By this time it was known that there would only be four further missions, and NASA tried to get the most from these. Most notable of the new equipment at their disposal was 'Rover', a 4-wheel drive vehicle which allowed astronauts from Apollo 15, 16 and 17 to explore the moon's surface, collecting a variety of rock samples. The Apollo program finished in December 1972, and man has yet to return to the surface of the moon.

"ONE SMALL STEP FOR MAN, ONE GIANT LEAP FOR MANKIND."

Apollo 11: Buzz Aldrin photographed by Neil Armstrong

Command module recovery

Twelve men have walked on the Moon, and one, Alan Shepard, has even played golf there!

the space SHUTTLE

The world's first reusable spacecraft, the US Space Shuttle, was first launched in 1981. It has three components – the Orbiter space plane, rocket boosters, and an external fuel tank – only the main fuel tank is not recovered after a mission. On the space plane's underside, special heat-resistant tiles prevent the Orbiter from burning up when it re-enters Earth's atmosphere. Astronauts use the large remote manipulator arm in the Orbiter's payload bay to deploy satellites into orbit, or recapture them from space for repair.

Each orbiter space plane has a name. The first was named Enterprise, after the spaceship in the famous TV series *Star Trek*. Built for test purposes, Enterprise never made it into space, but it did make a number of trial flights – taken to an altitude of 22,000ft (6,770m) on top of a Boeing 747 jet before being released to glide safely back to Earth.

There are four Orbiters in the present shuttle fleet: Columbia, Discovery, Atlantis and Endeavour. On 28 January 1986, to the horror of millions of television viewers, another shuttle, Challenger, exploded less than two minutes after launch. It was totally destroyed, and all seven crew members were killed. A seal in the booster rocket had failed, causing a gas leak, which then ignited. The Shuttle programme was stopped for three years while safety was improved.

Enjoying zero gravity aboard Columbia

Safely back to Earth

HL-10 early test prototype

The Space Shuttle can carry 29 tonnes of cargo into space.

exploration SPACE

DID YOU KNOW?

... that Polish lawyer Nicolaus Copernicus revolutionised astronomy in the early 16th century with his view that the sun was at the centre of the universe and not the earth.

... that our exploration into space really started with the Sputnik 1 satellite in 1957.

... that to escape the pull of earth's gravity, a rocket needs to achieve a high speed velocity of nearly 25,000mph.

... that in 1961 a Russian cosmonaut, Yuri Gagarin, became the first man in space.

... that Alexei Leonov made the first space walk in March 1965.

... that the first ever landing on the Moon was made by the Russian Luna 9 unmanned lander in 1966.

... that Neil Armstrong became the first man to walk on the moon in July 1969.

... that footprints left by astronauts walking on the moon's surface will still be there in 10 million years, as there is no weather.

... that in 1970 Venera 7 became the first lander to transmit data from the surface of Venus.

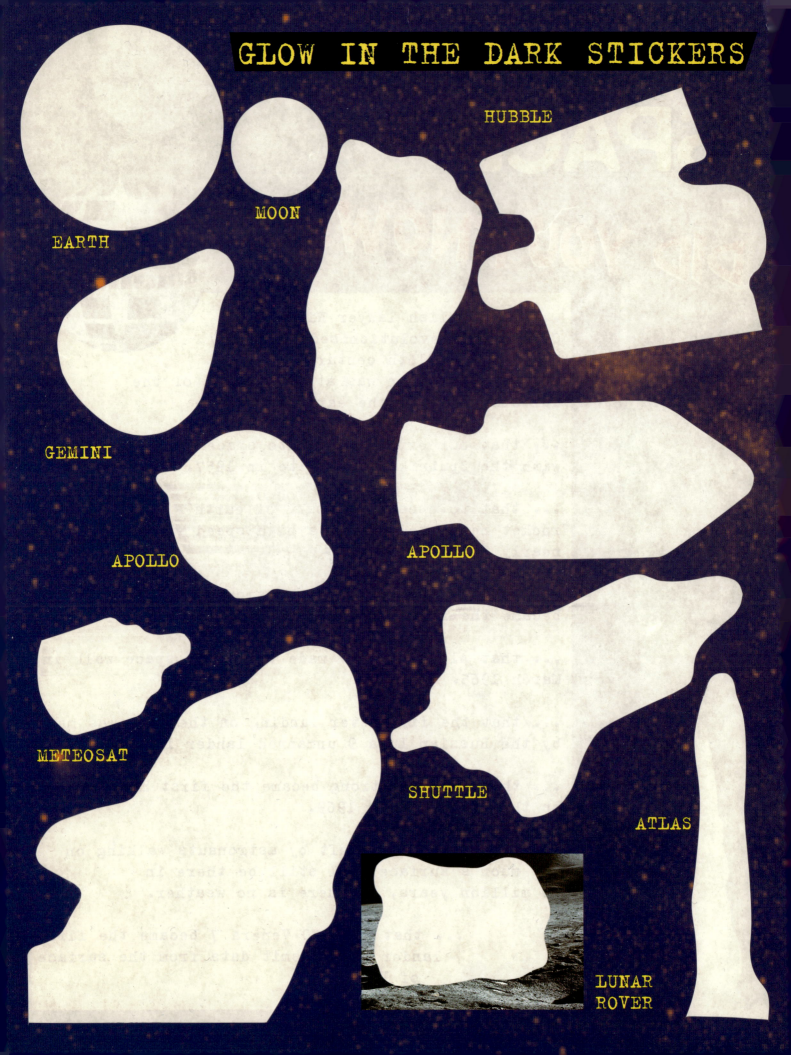

exploration
SPACE

DID YOU KNOW?

... that every year over 27,000 tonnes of extraterrestrial material enters the earth's atmosphere.

... that the world's largest radio telescope (the Arecibo dish in Puerto Rico) has a huge diameter of 1,000ft.

... that the most travelled spacecraft is the American Pioneer 10 which has, so far, journeyed over 6.5 billion miles (10.5 billion kilometres).

... that the longest space flight, 437 days, was made by Russian Valeri Poliakov in the *Mir* space station.

... that in space it is possible to sleep standing upright, as there is no up or down.

... that astronauts enjoy Coca Cola on the space shuttle thanks to specially adapted cans.

... that 400 people have ventured into space in 210 missions, 123 USA and 87 Russian flights.

... that plans are being made for a space hotel with sports and other leisure facilities and, of course, rooms with a mega view!

... that the Pioneer deep space probes carry images of human beings as well as simple directions for locating Earth.

SPACE SHUTTLES HAVE FLOWN OVER 50 SUCCESSFUL MISSIONS

LIFT OFF!

Satellite deployment and repair is the shuttle's main function

SPACE FAX

THE SPACE SHUTTLE has 34,000 heat shield tiles fixed to its underside for protection during re-entry, when they heat up to 1,600 degrees Celsius

The vast shuttle launch site at Cape Canaveral in Florida

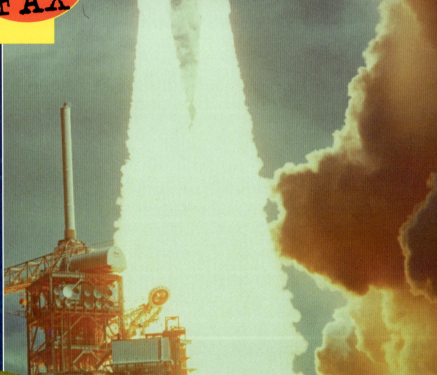

The Shuttle's two reusable booster rockets burn for two minutes before being jettisoned.

Sputnik 1 – the first satellite

Below: Launched in July 1962, Telstar transmitted the first live television pictures between the USA and Europe

SATELLITES

When Telstar sent the first live TV pictures across the Atlantic people were amazed. Since then thousands of satellites have been put into orbit around the earth. A great many of them are still there hurtling around. Powered by large 'wings' of solar panels, they are used for a variety of different purposes.

Communications satellites keep us up to date with TV pictures from around the world, they link us to mobile phones, faxes, pagers and keep computers talking to each other. Some can deal with up to 30,000 phone, data and fax calls at one time.

Weather satellites constantly monitor the earth's atmosphere relaying vital facts and information to weather forecasters around the world. This allows the weather men to warn us of impending hurricanes or predict droughts more accurately than ever before.

Some satellites monitor the earth's pollution, rainforest destruction, giving details about the seas and oceans, and making sophisticated maps of the earth's surface.

Explorer 6

Left: Explorer 6 sent back the first picture of earth from space

Below: Satellites have small rocket thrusters fitted, so they can be repostioned in space

TIROS 1 – the first weather satellite

Old rocket stages, nuts and bolts and other debris also orbit Earth ...

Syncom IV

Thanks to the Shuttle, work on satellites is carried out in space

ERS-1 monitors the Earth's resources

Infra-red satellite photograph of San Francisco.

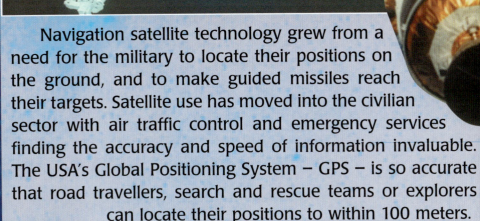

Navigation satellite technology grew from a need for the military to locate their positions on the ground, and to make guided missiles reach their targets. Satellite use has moved into the civilian sector with air traffic control and emergency services finding the accuracy and speed of information invaluable. The USA's Global Positioning System – GPS – is so accurate that road travellers, search and rescue teams or explorers can locate their positions to within 100 meters. Perhaps the most famous satellite working for us is the Hubble Space Telescope, put into orbit in 1990 and serviced by the Space Shuttle. Hubble can 'see' 10 times further than any earth-based telescopes, allowing astronomers to observe the most amazing images from deep space.

Meteosat

SATELLITES BRING US INSTANT GLOBAL COMMUNICATIONS

Communications satellites use dish antennae to send signals around the world

THE HUBBLE SPACE TELESCOPE is over 42ft (13m) long and its primary mirror took five years to make. It can see images 14 billion light years away

SPACE FAX

... these fast-moving pieces of space junk can be a real hazard to satellites and space stations.

13

space STATIONS

In 1971 the Soviet Union's Salyut 1 became the first space station. The Salyut series finished 11 years later with Salyut 7 (pictured below)

Besides the dream of landing men on the moon, writers, film makers and scientists have often imagined living in space – not just for a few days, but for weeks, months, even years.

Having lost the moon race, the Russian teams continued their research to develop an orbiting space station. In April 1971 they launched Salyut 1, which allowed a 3 man crew from Soyuz 10 to dock with and occupy Salyut 1 for 5 hours, becoming the first space station residents. The Salyut program continued until April 1982 with several missions including the 1975 link-up between the Soyuz and Apollo 18 astronauts, sealed by the historic handshake in space.

Meantime the Americans were having great success with Skylab. Using leftover Apollo technology Skylab, launched in April 1973, was home to three different crews of astronauts and scientists. The first crew had to repair some early damage to the station which occurred during its launch. When the work was complete they were able to use their unique position in space to observe and photograph the Earth, to study the sun, planets and stars, to carry out anti-gravity experiments. Their longest mission lasted 84 days.

Left: America put its first space station, Skylab, into orbit in 1973. Losing one of its solar panels during the launch, another panel was later deployed which saved the mission

Mir space station

Skylab space station was made from a spare Saturn V rocket stage ...

The International Space Station should be completed in 2004 and will be the size of a small town

After the Skylab program ended Russian Salyut space stations continued to play host to crews staying for longer and longer spells in space. This work paved the way for the more recent Mir space station.

The first stage was launched in February 1986, over the next few years further sections were flown up and added. More spacious than earlier stations, Salyut had room for exercising, sleeping bunks and washing facilities.

These 'normal' comforts feature on the Space Shuttle. USA's very successful reusable spacecraft, will be supplying the new ISS – International Space Station – for development over the next decade. The ISS will look like a small town upon completion.

SPACE FAX
MIR space station smashed every space endurance record in the book, including longest ever space flight (437 days)

The International Space Station (ISS) currently under development

... Skylab crews took over 40,000 photographs of the Earth from their laboratory in space.

deep space PROBES

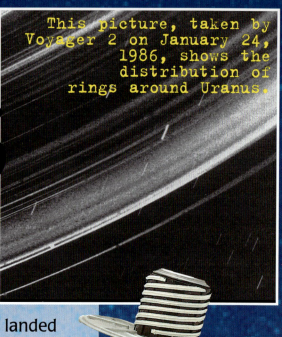
This picture, taken by Voyager 2 on January 24, 1986, shows the distribution of rings around Uranus.

Since the early 1960s unmanned probes have been launched by the USA and USSR, with the one aim of collecting information about our Solar System. Since then each planet except Pluto has been observed, photographed, and in some cases even landed on, to discover something about its composition, atmosphere and temperature. The sun has also been observed by several probes including some Pioneer spacecraft, and the recently launched SOHO will conduct non-stop observations.

In 1973 Mariner 10 showed amazing pictures of Mercury and its meteorite cratered surface. In 1975 the USSR's Veneras 9 and 10 orbited and photographed Venus.

Probes were sent to the moon, before and after the manned landings, but Mars has always been the planet which holds most interest. The Mariner program orbited and photographed Mars, while in 1976 two Viking craft landed and took samples of martian soil. The Later Pathfinder spacecraft landed a roving vehicle for more surface exploration. Now everyone is waiting for a craft that can collect rock samples and return them to earth. Further away from Earth, Jupiter became the object of the Galileo space probe. Galileo sent back data of Jupiter's thick cloudy atmosphere as the ship descended, toward the planet's surface.

In 1997, controlled by radio signals from Earth, Sojourner roams the Martian surface

Venera lander

The Soviet Venera series have sent back data about Venus

The Galileo probe lasted less than an hour, in Jupiter's hostile atmosphere

Viking I takes the first picture on Mars.

exploration SPACE info

Voyager and Pioneer probes use the planets' gravitational pull ...

WHAT REALLY LIES BEYOND THE SOLAR SYSTEM?

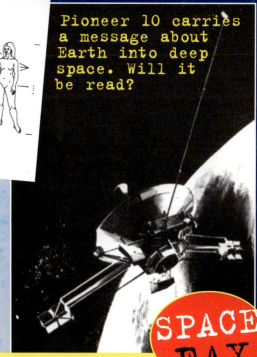

Pioneer 10 carries a message about Earth into deep space. Will it be read?

This was not the first time Jupiter had been visited; some years before, it had been passed by one of the four deep space probes that we have sent out into the unknown depths of space.

We have so much to discover about our own Solar System but still can't help wondering what is beyond, whether there are other civilisations out there. When the Pioneer 10 probe was launched in 1972, an opportunity to communicate in the simplest way was not missed. Pioneer had a small metal plaque on its side that showed in outline a man, a woman and a map of how to find our planet Earth. This probe is heading towards the star Aldebaran, and should reach it in two million years time. A year later Pioneer 11 was launched, this probe should take four million years, to reach its destination, the distant constellation Aquila.

Four years after Pioneer 11, the two Voyager probes were launched. On its way past Jupiter, Voyager 1 sent back beautiful photographs of the planet's swirling atmosphere, including the famous red spot, and also showed an active volcano on Jupiter's moon, Io. Twelve years after its launch Voyager 2 was able to send back pictures of Saturn and to show that Uranus had at least 15 moons, this information only took four hours, travelling at the speed of light to reach earth. Both Voyagers carried on past their target planets and out of our Solar System; Voyager 1 is heading for the constellation of Camelpardus which it should reach in 400,000 years time. Voyager 2's destination is Sirius, 8.6 light years from Earth and currently the brightest star in the night sky. It should pass close by Sirius just before Voyager 1 reaches its goal.

SPACE FAX

PIONEER 10 is heading for the star Aldebaran - it will take 2 million years to get there!

Below: Voyager 1 took this amazing close-up picture of Jupiter's swirling atmosphere

... to change course and head out of the solar system into the far unknown of deep space.

the FUTURE?

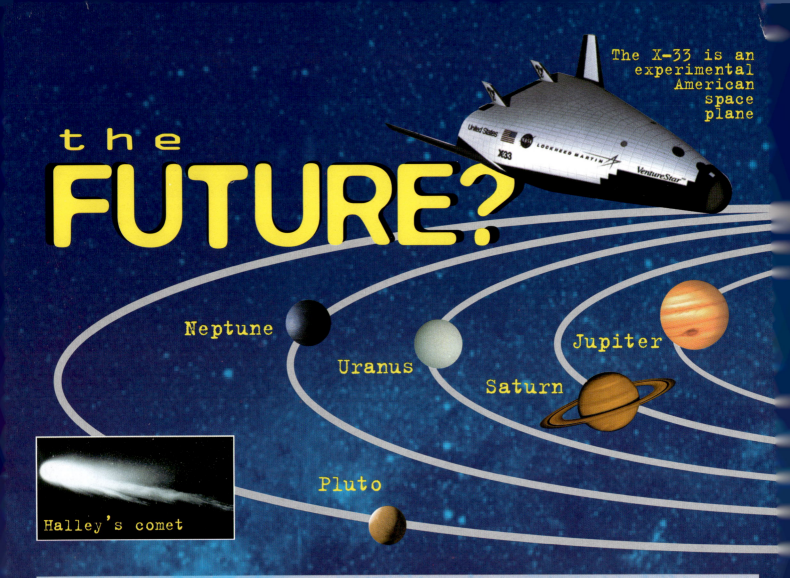

The X-33 is an experimental American space plane

Neptune Uranus Saturn Jupiter Pluto

Halley's comet

WHERE WILL WE TRAVEL TO NEXT?

As we have already seen, deep space probes are heading out past the furthermost planets of our solar system. Travelling any real distance is not likely for humans in the near future, our next journeys will be confined to those planets which are nearest to Earth.

Plans for a manned mission to Mars still exist, both the Americans and the Russians possess the technology to develop flight and landing craft for the mission. At present there is no money to pay for this very costly project. It would take between four and nine months for a vehicle to reach Mars, to deploy a Lander craft and enter the Martian atmosphere to land on the planet's surface. Astronauts could explore the ground in roving vehicles, taking readings and collecting rock samples. It might even be possible for astronauts to make their own fuel for the return journey using methane and oxygen from the Martian atmosphere.

There is also the possibility of manned space stations on the Moon. International co-operation might make mining

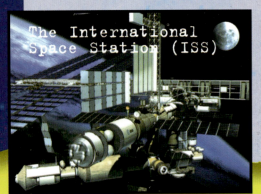

The International Space Station (ISS)

With many thousands of galaxies still waiting to be explored ...

the planet Mars may well prove to be inhabitable

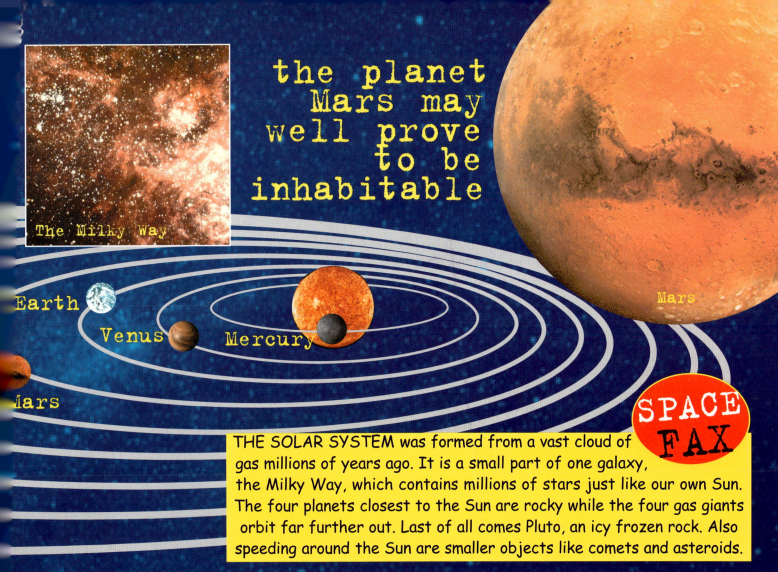

The Milky Way

Earth
Venus
Mercury
Mars
Mars

SPACE FAX

THE SOLAR SYSTEM was formed from a vast cloud of gas millions of years ago. It is a small part of one galaxy, the Milky Way, which contains millions of stars just like our own Sun. The four planets closest to the Sun are rocky while the four gas giants orbit far further out. Last of all comes Pluto, an icy frozen rock. Also speeding around the Sun are smaller objects like comets and asteroids.

stations, space telescopes or even lunar hotels possible within the next 20 years. Moon bases could provide a starting point for trips to further planets in our solar system.

Most likely, however, is the establishment of orbiting space stations, built with the co-operation of the United States, Russia, Japan and some European countries. An International Space Station (ISS) is currently being built to orbit the Earth. This would be used for scientific study, research and tourism – some travel companies are already selling flights on future space shuttles and even planning visits to orbiting space hotels. These will be reached by space planes such as the proposed Horus craft, launched from the back of a huge 150 ton reusable hypersonic first stage rocket. See you there for a holiday that's out of this world!

Below: The German Saenger project features a reusable rocket to launch the smaller Horus space plane

... can we really be sure that we are alone in the universe?

SEE SPACESHIPS GLOWING IN YOUR ROOM!

"A small step for a man, one giant leap for mankind."

SPACE, THE FINAL FRONTIER...

FROM EARLY ROCKETS TO THE HUBBLE SPACE TELESCOPE AND DEEP SPACE PROBES...

IN 'EXPLORATION SPACE', YOU'LL TRAVEL TO THE FAR REACHES OF THE UNIVERSE!

OTHER TITLES IN THE GLOW-IN-THE-DARK SERIES:
- DINOSAURS • UNDERSEA
- BUGS • WEATHER
- BUTTERFLIES • UFO
- PLANETS • SHARK

Author & Design: John Starke
Development: Martin Rhodes-Schofield

Copyright ©2000 Red Bird Publishing Ltd.
Brightlingsea Colchester Essex CO7 0SX England
www.red-bird.co.uk
All rights reserved. Printed in England

£3.99 UK
$5.95 US

ISBN 1-902626-25-7